Legends of Altai

BOOK 2

Chronicles of King Ultan

Written by Paolo F. Tiberi

Published by Effective Life Strategies Pty Ltd
www.effectivelifestrategies.com

Copyright © 2010 by Paolo F. Tiberi All right reserved

No part of this book is to be reproduced by any mechanical, photographic, electronic process, or in the form of a phonographic recording. It may not be stored in any retrieval system, transmitted, and copied for public or private use without consent from the author – other than for *"fair use"* as brief quotations in the embodiment of articles or reviews.

The author of this book does not dispense medical advice or prescribe the use of any technique as a form of treatment for any physical, mental or emotional problem. The author has two intents with this book: 1) To offer a book with stories to open one's mind and heart so it may rekindle the inner fire contained within the soul. 2) To help individuals in their quest for spiritual well-being and developing a more fulfilled life.

A CIP catalog record for this book is available from the Australian Library
Author: Tiberi, Paolo F.
Title: Chronicles of King Ultan
written by Paolo F. Tiberi.
ISBN: 978-1-921851-11-7 (pbk.)
Series: Legends of Altai - Book 2
Audience: For primary school age and older
(Adults love the stories too!)

Contents

1. An Important Letter to Parents 05

2. How to get the best out of this book......................07

3. About Altai...11

4. The King and the Miraculous Healing....................13

5. The King and the Beggar...28

6. King Ultan and his 3 sons..37

7. Looking Inside..53

8. Work-Book for Students..64

9. Coloring Book …..98

10. Teachers/Parents Reference Book......................101

11. Connect, share this book with others................127

AN IMPORTANT LETTER TO PARENTS

Dear Parents,

We all come from different cultural backgrounds, religions, and belief systems. However, the stories in this book can easily be adapted to fit any personal viewpoint. I believe it is better to equip our children with some form of self-awareness, wisdom, and knowledge than none at all.

We live in a society where our children have been unconsciously trained to disassociate themselves from feelings of compassion, empathy, or guilt. False heroes found in most video games, television shows, internet and movies often set this silent training.

Many of our leaders have forgotten that you cannot have a functional, balanced and caring society without functional children, therefore they allow this silent training to be ever present.

In a society where instant gratification has replaced true labour and dedication, children have grown to expect everything immediately. They want instant soup instead of a finely brewed broth, even though the latter is more flavorsome and better for them.

It is sad that we have found ourselves living in a world where success is measured by how many "toys" one possesses. Kids are subtly and passively trained to desire materialistic things more and more, and never feel content.

We do have a way to step in and give our children positive guidance for a more enriching future.

Through your life, your words and actions and through the gifts (like this little book) you give your child, you have the ability to make a positive, profound choice for your child's life. You can become their beacon of light by teaching them to become loving, caring, and wiser beings. This is what the true gifts of life are about.

I ask you to help us change society one small child at the time through this little book of wisdom.

I hope that after having read these stories, you will feel that they are worth sharing.

How to get the best out of this book

This book is for both adults and children alike. Every person has the ability to learn valuable lessons when they open up their hearts and minds.

I grew up hearing great ancient stories and parables that have helped me with my own personal growth and life. It is my wish to share these stories with you in the hope that they will live in your heart. As you grow older I believe you will pass them on from generation to generation. Wisdom and a solid foundation in life are the gifts that will keep on giving.

There is no better opportunity to bond with your child than by sharing tales that intrigue them and invite questions on life. This will help them internalize the message, lesson, and wisdom for themselves. That internalization will create the seed of true self-awareness that all people need to prosper in their daily experiences.

The best way to absorb the benefits of this book is to slow down. Take time to savour each story. When you read them, make sure you listen to what the tale is telling you within the realms of not only your mind, but also your heart. We often forget how wise our hearts can be, too.

After you complete a story, there are a few questions you and your child could reflect upon:

* How did this story touch me?
* Did this tale awaken anything inside me?
* How could I use the message to positively affect or better my life and/or others?
* Is there any aspect of my life that needs the kind of understanding and healing addressed in the story?

It is impossible to read the tales in this book and not form a personal relationship with each one of them. Some of the stories may have a more profound effect on you than others, but the more you read them, the more you will find the different levels of meaning within each one.

Since people all react differently to the messages in these tales, they can become great tools to start communication with those around you. Some of you may want to laugh or cry. Others will simply be touched by the message of the story. In the end, there is neither a right nor wrong reaction. Rather, there is an opportunity to learn about your true self and open up the doors to discussions about life and its choices with your children, friends, or family.

Let each one of these stories flow through your mind, heart and self freely. Contemplate on the messages learned, and if you can feel that it has moved you, make sure to share it with others.

Everyone can benefit from your self-realization and perhaps inspire others to emulate the messages learnt. You have the unlimited potential to reach out and touch somebody, either by calling them, emailing them, or writing a letter to let them know that you have learned or have been reminded of something amazing.

Since the goal is for every child to relate to these stories with a universal message, the word "God" has been changed to "The Great One" to make it easier to accept.

FREE GIFTS IN THIS BOOK:
1. Parent/Teacher & Student Workbook for story 1.
2. A coloring book, containing all of the main characters.

To see availability of Book 1, 3 and 4 please visit:
www.legendsofaltai.com

About Altai

The Altai Mountains are one of the most serene, secluded and beautiful locations on Earth. They remain that way because of their exclusiveness and limited accessibility.

The name Altai has origins from the word Altan; which means golden mountains in the Mongolian dialect. Altai lies securely in a mountain range in central Asia that stretches for 2,000 kilometers and forms a natural border between Russia, China, Mongolia and Kazakhstan.

There has never been another place like Altai since anyone can remember; where extraordinary events, spirituality, and mysticism meet common life. A land that some people believe is a doorway between heaven and earth attracting seekers of spiritual enlightenment into its realm for countless millennia.

For more information on the mystical place called Altai, please visit: www.legendsofaltai.com

1. King Argoz and the Miraculous Healing

The sun was rising and glistening on the crispy white snow that winter morning. Inside the castle, a new little prince named Ultan was born into the royal family. King Argoz had waited for a male heir to the throne for a long time. The King paced the castle halls until he was called in to view his new son.

The King looked down with anticipation and froze in his tracks. This child is deformed and surely cannot be the long awaited heir to Argoz' throne. He began crying and yelling, "Why has the Great One looked upon me so unfavorably? My Kingdom needs a strong and mighty heir to the throne!"

Argoz called all the doctors and physicians in his Kingdom to come. He demanded they heal the child, but it was to no avail.

As the years passed by, no doctor was able to cure the young Ultan. Even the most respected healers from faraway lands to tried, but nobody could heal the boy. The infant grew to be a child. He could not play with other children because he was very frail and could not walk properly. Therefore, Ultan spent most of his time in the palace library. He learned to read at a very young age and absorbed many great words of wisdom that lived within the library walls.

After eleven years had passed, the King had all but given up hope. Every time he saw his son, he thought of how he still didn't have an heir to his throne. Such a frail man could never be a leader.

The King remembered the lesson of the blue violet bush, but he struggled to find the strength to come to terms with his son's condition.

As a last effort, the King invited the wisest people to his castle. Both wise men and women came to court to offer their assistance. These great beings were from all areas of the world. That very moment the palace reception contained more knowledge than it had ever had before. Yet, these brilliant wise people could not heal Ultan.

One of the men called Xavier the Wise looked to the shaken King kindly. "Dear King, you might not know why this has happened to your son although it may seem like a curse to you at the moment, there might be a reason for it. Perhaps the Great One does not feel it is yet time for you to understand it. Remember that the ways of the Creator are strange and bizarre at times and not one of us can truly foresee the greatness of his invisible plans however, if you truly seek to uncover the Great One's plan for your child, go to the highest mountain peak in your Kingdom by yourself. You must fully surrender and show true humility as you seek for the Great One's assistance. If you have trust, I believe help will be provided."

Willing to try anything to ensure a great heir for his Kingdom, the King decided to follow the wise man's advice. He began his journey to the mountain top. He was weary when he reached the top, but exerted great strength to call for the Great One. King Argoz lifted his arms to the sky and said, "Great One, creator of all things, I am the King of this land. I wish for you to heal my son."

The King waited for an answer. He was very still and afraid to breathe, lest he miss a sign from the Great One. No answer came. He was discouraged, but decided not to leave. He set up camp. As he waited he recollected what the wise man said. He recalled that he needed to be truly humble. So, after a night of camping on the cold mountain peak, the King reached out to the Great One again.

"Great One, you have power over all things. I humbly submit to you and ask that you use your great power to heal my deformed son. My Kingdom needs a strong heir to the throne."

Again no answer came. King Argoz called out again, "Please Great One, I have failed to have more sons. The only heir to my mighty Kingdom is disabled and cannot lead. I beg you, heal him…"

He received only deep silence that was eerily still and calm. The King felt deeply dejected. He sensed just how futile his prayers and actions were at that moment. He did not understand how such a powerful King as he was had no power to heal his son. The more the King thought, the weaker he became. He knew not what to do, but did not want to give up.

The King wept uncontrollably. His chest pounded with pain with every heartbeat. He felt that he would collapse under the weight of his sorrows. The sun had set behind the mountaintops again. The air grew colder just like the night before. This time the snow came down and the King's body began to shake. He dropped to the ground unable to get back up. His tears fell and froze to his eyelashes and cheeks. He then removed his shoes and all his royal garments until he stood before the Great One stripped down to nothing.

King Argoz was completely exposed and tried to pray once again. He surrendered and could no longer take the pain.

"Great One, creator of all things, I do not understand your ways. I come to you as a man, as you have made me. I do not speak to you as a King or a lawmaker. I speak to you as a simple man who is powerless and without knowledge or means to help my son. As your child, can you not understand why I wish to help my own son? If it is your will to keep my son the way he is, may your will stand and my request be ignored. I am ready to accept it. I do not pretend to know the reasoning behind your great wisdom, but I do trust that you know the best possible life and destiny for me and my son. Please help my Kingdom find an heir if it is not to be Ultan."

Broken with heartache and exhaustion, the King got dressed again. He slowly made his way down the mountain and his frozen tears began to thaw, yet he did not stop crying.

As he stopped for a rest, a deep voice came from within and said, "Dear King, listen carefully. The people, places and events in your life have been chosen by your own soul. The soul of your son and its decisions are a stepping stone on the path to his healing and awakening. I have created a field of potential and opportunity for the two of you so that you may experiment and grow wiser."

"I do not understand, Great One."

"Ultan, your son is a great soul. He has decided that he will dedicate his youth to learning all he can without any outside distraction that's why he created his physical manifestation the way it is now. Everything has a reason and a higher purpose behind it. He has learned the power of self-transformation through creative thought. Not only will he become a wise King, but he will also be a great teacher and healer. His soul created his journey. I just provided the backdrop for his creation."

"How can this be when he is disabled and weak?" the King wondered.

"You must see beyond the physical presence of this world and look deeper into it. The only true disability is a close heart and a close, limited mind. Most people that you refer to as 'normal' are heart and soul-disabled. Disability dear Argoz, is a matter of perception, individuals with disability have achieved great feats and have become inspiring, dynamic and capable beings. Your son's disability does not stop him from becoming a great and just ruler. In fact the biggest limitation your son has is what you put upon him, by thinking he will not be able to rule. Remember the lesson of the Blue Violet. Everyone has a unique purpose in life no matter who they are or what condition they are born in.* Everyone matters. However your son's destiny is to show that his will and desire are stronger than any human limitation.

Your son is ready for his true form to unfold. Therefore, to help your son transform his appearance, you need to build a statue outside his bedroom window. It needs to be exactly as you envision your son to be without his current disabilities. See him the way you wish him to - strong, tall, and wise."

"I will do that. What do I do after the statue is built, Great One?" King Argoz asked.

"Ask your son to look at the statue every morning after awaking and every night before going to sleep and whenever he wants in between.

*Refer to our official website for inspiring true-life videos and stories. Link:

http://www.legendsofaltai.com/true-life-stories/

Tell him that this is how he will grow up to be by his eighteenth birthday. Tell him that he needs to envision himself like the statue for as long as possible every day. He cannot let the distracting thoughts of this world interrupt him. Tell him to finish the exercise with gratitude, and to exclaim, 'It is done, so be it!' Little by little, his soul will imprint a new dream on his body and mind and his body will adapt to its own intent and dream," replied the Great One.

The King nodded. He was beginning to understand.

"My dear King, everything that you see and don't see is made up of my energy and my love. This free flow of energy merely awaits dreamers to put in their creative thought or imagination for it to move, materialize and turn it into reality."

The voice continued, "The idea is to present your son with a new possibility that he can really become excited about. Then as he dreams this new possibility each day, the more he will accept this as reality. Soon, his dream will be made law and it will come to pass. Always remember, no limitations have been placed on my sons' and daughters' creative powers. Whatever you truly desire will be given to you if you ask for it with complete acceptance, belief, and surrender."

"Go now and never forget the lessons you have learned on this mountain," continued the Great One.

The King descended down the mountain.

He came down a changed man. In his eyes you could see new wisdom, humility and strength clearly showing through.

He did what was asked of him and told young Ultan about the experience on the mountain with the Great One.

Ultan smiled at him with eyes wiser than his young years.

By the day of Ultan's eighteenth birthday, he was a transformed young man. His body was as strong as the statue outside his window. Because of a youth spent in study and contemplation, he was also one of the wisest man in the Kingdom.

Ultan passed on his wisdom and knowledge to all who wished to receive it.

He taught all who wanted to hear about the great power of one's self and about what he had done. He always finished his talks with a quote, which he loved best. "The Great One once said to my father 'No limitations have been placed on my sons' and daughters' creative powers. Whatever you truly desire will be given to you. All you need to do is ask for it with complete acceptance, belief and surrender.' Therefore, as citizens of this land, it is time to go and make your dreams a reality, much like the way an artist paints on his canvas of life using the brilliant colors of creation!"

The Kingdom flourished. Knowledge, love, compassion and discipline were abundant amongst the people. The citizens became wiser and the discoveries and miracles they made were great.

Even people from other places came to visit the land to see and learn.

2. King Ultan and the Beggar

As King Ultan continued with the help of his sister, Princess Maya to govern the Kingdom his wisdom grew. His desire for learning attracted many great teachers, wizards and healers.

One day, the king decided to do what he liked best. That was to walk around the market place and see what the lands surrounding the kingdom had produced. It was always a good opportunity to talk with the people and ask what could be improved."

"King Ultan always felt satisfied to see the kingdom be productive. Talking with his citizens gave him an overall view of the economy and emotional state of his people. One day, in particular, King Ultan went around the market with his sister, Princess Maya."

"It was a beautiful day and the weather was great. Ultan noticed a beggar sitting alongside the street at the corner. He was curious because there were very few beggars in his kingdom. Therefore he decided to approached him. 'Tell me beggar, is there anything that you need? As king, I can fulfill any of your desires. All you need to do is ask. No person should be without food nor a roof over their head. The king looked at the beggar and was feeling very confident in his declaration."

"The beggar told the king that he couldn't satisfy his desires. The king didn't believe that to be so and said, 'Try me, beggar. After all, I am the king. I know that I can most certainly give you everything you want.' "

"The beggar said, 'My gracious king, I assure you that there is nothing that could fill this beggar's bowl. It cannot be done.' The beggar looked up to the king and smiled."

"The king started pouring copper coins in the bowl. Every coin that touched the bowl would instantly disappear. People from the market started gathering around to watch the scene. They wondered why things would disappear every time they touched the bowl. It must be a trick."

"The King continued to pour more coins, this time silver and even gold coins. He also added special gems. Yet, nothing worked. Each and Everything that touched the bowl would vanish. Eventually the king had nothing left to feed the bowl. This made him angry and disappointed. Confusion started to build within him. He could not figure out what magic this beggar has used with his bowl."

"The king tried to remain calm, although deep inside he was confused. 'Who are you? Is this a trick to steal the king's possessions?' He looked back down at the beggar, awaiting for an answer."

"No, my king, there is no trick and I have no desire to steal any of your kingdom's possessions. I am a teacher. You have asked to receive great wisdom and knowledge to guide your people and kingdom. I have come to help you make this wish a reality. I am here today to show you the nature of the human mind. This bowl is made of the same substance as your mind. Just like your mind, it can never be satisfied either. No matter what we desire, it is never enough thus we keep seeking for more."

"The wise teacher in beggar's clothes continued to share with the King. 'Our minds always want to focus on new goals and desires. It becomes a weapon to stop us from our higher purpose. The path to true inner peace and contentment comes from within. Once an individual starts focusing on what is within they will have found the answer to keeping their cup full with the best things in this world.' The king nodded at the man to continue."

"Dear King, this reminds us that there is nothing than does not exist in the now. The now is the only reality in existence and the rest is merely a projection in our minds. When we are young, we focus on the future, when we are old we become entranced by the past. Both are not real. One is mirage the other a ghost. "

"The king was now calm. He asked, 'Isn't desire necessary to fulfill our life purpose?' A crowd of people now sat around the great teacher waiting for his word and the king who was in the middle was waiting for an answer."

"The beggar smiled. 'Yes desire is necessary, but to answer that question fully, we need to first ask what the purpose of life truly is?' The teacher looked to the crowd for a reply to his question."

One woman said love. Another one agreed and added that making a contribution was important too. An old man believed that being successful in what you chose to do was important for the purpose of life.

The wise teacher looked to the crowd thoughtfully. He was not surprised by the answers since he'd heard them often.

He asked, 'Is success measured by money, recognition or something else?' He smiled and became silent.

"Princess Maya had been silent until that moment. 'No, they are not.' She said. Her eyes were on the ground and it was easy to see that she was thinking very intensely, trying to understand more."

"The teacher in beggar's clothes looked at Maya and offered a kind smile. He paused for a moment and then continued. 'That is correct. Money, wealth and possessions are temporary, they will never fully satisfy you. The life lessons learned and the wisdom obtained are the lasting treasures.' The teacher now stood up."

"He continued. 'In my many travels I discovered that deep inside people long for four things in life. The first is love.

The second is creation and purpose.

The third is knowledge and discovery.

And the fourth is contribution.

If love is missing in our life, then we feel empty. This love does not have to be limited to a partner but can be the love one feels for humanity, a son or daughter, or one's community, neighbours, or family.' The crowd was silent as they listened to the great teacher."

"If creation is missing we feel lost. As a reflection of our creator, the Great One, we feel the need to create. Again this could be a house, a book, a project, a child, or anything. Creation is part of our nature and without it we feel unfulfilled. Creation means that we have a purpose."

"If discovery, is missing, our life becomes dormant. There will be no challenges. There is no growth without new knowledge."

"If contribution is missing, life will seem to have no purpose. When we look at others achievements because of our contributions we can find true fulfillment. Once we realize that, we come to truly understand that others are a part of us. They are simply experimenting through another life experience."

"King Ultan thanked the wise teacher for his lesson and invited him to the castle for more conversation. The kind teacher smiled to the king and said, 'My purpose here is done today, Good King.

The teacher dressed in beggars clothes walked away through the crowd and towards the outskirts of town.

We turned back and said: "I will be back, there is much to learn and many more adventure to enjoy."

3. King Ultan and his 3 Sons

There once was a King known by all as Ultan. He was the son of the great King Argoz. He was blessed with three sons. They were triplets and were born only one minute apart.

He had to decide which of his three sons would one day take over the Kingdom. This was a dilemma that caused him great anxiety.

He didn't believe that the rule of the oldest son applied in this case. He wanted to find out which of his sons was the most just, wise and brave of heart. The people of his land deserved that type of King

The King invited the wise men and women of the land to seek their counsel and guidance as his father did before him. Surely these great men and women could help him decide which of his sons would be the most suitable to reign over the Kingdom.

As the wise men spoke, one by one they offered advice to the King and asked him questions. One wise old man asked, "Why don't you set up a test of bravery and strength?" The King did not like that idea. He was not looking for strength. He wanted an overall sense of justice, fairness, compassion and leadership from the future King.

Maya, Ultan's sister, who was renowned for her wisdom was also present. She had returned from her travels to help her brother for she knew how important it was to be governed by a wise and just King. Maya suggested a very good idea.

He called his sons at once. "Dear children, I am heading off on a pilgrimage to seek answers. I am not sure how long this journey will take. It could be a year, perhaps even longer. While I am gone the

Kingdom will be ruled by the 'round table.' The round table will be comprised of the three of you, your mother the Queen, Princess Maya, and a group of wise advisors."

The sons looked at their father curiously. They could not believe their father would abandon the Kingdom he loved so much for a pilgrimage. Because they honoured their father, they withheld their questions while he continued to speak.

"Each of you will be given a box of seeds.

The seeds are for fruit trees, ornamental tree, herbs, vegetables, and flowers. All these things grow and bloom throughout our entire region. In a year or more, I will be back and see what you have done with these seeds. Whichever one of you protects your seeds the best and makes the best use of them will be the rightful heir to the throne when I am no longer here. Do you understand, my sons?" Explained King Ultan.

The three sons nodded and knelt before their father in appreciation. They wanted to honour their father by being the best protector of the seeds.

Although all three sons looked very similar, they all thought very differently.

One of the sons called Aaron went and asked some farmers for the best way to preserve seeds. The farmers responded that if they were kept in a cool area with no humidity the seeds should preserve well for several years without fear of rotting. He decided to follow the farmer's advice and that it would be wise to lock the seeds in a secured box.

He placed that box in a cool, dry place and wrapped it in layers of cloth to help prevent any humidity from seeping in. When his father returned, he would give him the valuable seeds back.

The second son, Niall, thought for days about what he should do. After careful consideration he decided to go to the market place to sell the seeds.

With the money from the sale of the seeds, he would invest it to earn more. Upon his father's return, he would take the money and purchase even more seeds to present to his father. He felt most confident that these wise choice would help him get the crown.

The third son, Ryan, decided to plant the seeds in the royal fields.

They would create both beauty throughout the Kingdom and a productive oasis.

As time went by, the seeds grew into small trees, flowers, herbs, vegetables, and fruit. Ryan kept harvesting the seeds and used them to plant more. The Kingdom kept growing more beautiful and was rich in resources for all the people of the Kingdom. As you looked across the land you could see the beautiful colors of the blossoming flowers and lush plants. The air was filled with the sweet fragrance of bountifulness.

To show his loyalty to the Kingdom he took one extra step. He let it be known that any willing family could harvest from the oasis on one condition. They needed to reap any extra seeds they had after growing their own food and provide those seeds to other families to use. No seed that produced life and food should be discarded. They were to be used for its intended purpose.

Three years soon passed by. The King finally returned and all the people rejoiced at the sight of him. It was a great day and the entire Kingdom was preparing a feast to celebrate the return of their great King.

Niall, after learning that the King had returned, ran to the market and purchased nearly double the amount of seeds he had started with. His money grew great interest over those three years. He was very proud and hoped his father would see how clever he was. One thing the second son noticed was that the roads of the Kingdom looked more lush and colorful than they had ever been before.

Once settled back in the Kingdom, the King called his three sons to appear before him. He had missed them and was very intrigued to hear about how they had used their seeds.

Before the King listened to his sons, he said, "Dear sons, there are no right or wrong ways when it comes to these seeds. Every one of you has done the best you could do, based on the way you perceive life. A chef would see water as a beautiful tool for great creations and as an indispensable ingredient for many of his recipes. A farmer may look at water as a tool for growing his crops and creating life. Engineers would view water as a way to produce endless energy. People use the gift of water differently. All ways are good and necessary to better one's life. Therefore, do not be discouraged if you are not chosen to become the King. Each of you will have a purpose and fulfil a precious role in this Kingdom."

"Wouldn't one be more important than another?" Aaron asked.

"Dear one, can the heart survive in a body without a stomach? Or can the nose and breathing exist in a body without a lung? They cannot. All of the parts are integral for the system to work. One needs the other to work together effectively. Everyone plays an important role in life, whether they are a cleaner, teacher, doctor or a leader. We all need each other for the whole system to work properly. Every one matters."

"The test with the seeds, is not just about determining who will become King. It is also about learning your path in life," explained King Ultan.

The King smiled tenderly. Then he asked his sons to show him their results one by one.

Aaron got the box of seeds his father had given him and opened the box. King Ultan looked at the well-preserved seeds. He hugged his son and said: "My son, you have done well. It looks like you would take good care of managing our produce and crops that are harvested in the Kingdom. Thank you for your great effort. I am proud."

Niall opened a bigger container showcasing double the amount of seeds. The King asked, "Son, are these my seeds?"

"No, father. I sold your seeds and reinvested the money from the seeds. Upon your arrival back to the Kingdom, I ran to the market and purchased double the seeds with the money I had earned."

The King hugged Niall and said, "You, my son, are a great visionary with seeing the potential of things and helping them to grow. You would take great care in managing the Kingdom treasury. Thank you for your great effort. You have made me proud."

The King looked to the third son, Ryan. "What did you do with your seeds, son?"

Ryan asked his father to follow him outside. He showed him the royal fields and gardens. "Those, my King, are the fruit of your seeds. The Kingdom is now producing fruit for both the court and the people of the Kingdom. The extra seeds that the trees, vegetables, herbs, and ornamental flowers have created were distributed to families around the Kingdom with only one condition. They must share the seeds their plants generated with others so that they, too, may have food. The seeds are gifts that will keep on giving for all time. I do not have any seeds with me at the moment as all had been sowed to give life to new plants.

However, if you be patient a bit longer all the plants will produce their fruit and their seeds can be harvested."

The King embraced his son. "You, my son, will be a great King and leader! You have shown everyone that the idea of one single man can change an entire Kingdom!"

The seeds of the earth that grew within King Ultan's flourishing Kingdom continued to give. It is said that the Kingdom lived in great abundance. As friends and relatives from neighbouring Kingdoms visit, they would be given seeds to take back to their homes. Their only condition was the one that had initially been set by the young prince. Any excess seeds were to be given to others for free. All of the citizens of the Kingdom organised to give the seeds to villagers of other Kingdoms. The visitors delivered the seeds. Now, Kingdoms far and wide flourished with bountiful harvests and fruit.

Visitors to the Kingdom were always astounded and entranced by the richness, prosperity and beauty of the Kingdom. Ryan was truly a great leader. Visitors decided to replicate what they had done in this Kingdom in their own homelands. They too wanted to create such beauty, bounty and giving.

It has been proven that the idea of one single young man can change not only a single Kingdom, but also the entire planet. In fact, Planet Earth became a Garden of Eden once again. This was because of the simple yet magnificent idea of a young prince.

4. Looking Inside

Out on the eastern regions of King Ultan's Kingdom sat a small village. It barely stood out among the vast land and mountain ranges. Sixty people lived in this small village. It stood isolated because there were no proper roads going in or out. So, the villagers relied on the land to provide them food, shelter, and everything else they needed. They counted on mules and horses for transportation.

As of late, something had made the people in the village grow increasingly anxious. The situation was made worse by a desire for the villagers to compete with each other. It started out of boredom, but grew into a restless discontent and actions that were unkind. Where there was once harmony, there was now hostility. The little village was no longer serene. In fact, it was becoming increasingly unpleasant. People no longer enjoyed living there.

Malariba was one of the wisest elders in the village. She sat back under her hut canopy. Her face was weathered from the intense sun, but her eyes had the alertness of a newborn. She knew that she must do something about the village's behaviour to save its precious traditions.

One evening as night slowly fell upon the village, Malariba made her way to the main road on the outskirts of the village. She carefully kneeled down to the ground and began searching for something. Since everyone in the village was congregated, Malariba caught their attention. The villagers were curious.

"What are you looking for, Malariba?" a curious girl from the village asked.

"I have lost my most precious gem," said Malariba.

One young man in particular took interest. He beckoned his fellow villagers to gather around him.

Everybody began to look for the valuable, precious and treasured gem that Malariba had lost.

Their competitive spirit made them focus more on the hopes of a reward than on the kindness of a good deed. As the villagers search continued, the sun slowly set in the distant horizon. It was becoming very difficult to look for such a small gem.

One of the most competitive elderly men in the village turned to Malariba. "What does the gem look like exactly?"

"Like a big diamond." You could hear the whispers amongst the crowd of villagers. They liked the sound of that and wished to be the one to find it first. Surely there would be a reward for the return of such a valuable treasure.

"Where exactly do you remember seeing it last?" asked another man determined to be the one to find the precious stone.

Malariba smiled. "In my house."

Aggravation stirred in the crowd. What was Malariba up to?

"Have you gone crazy, old lady? Why would you have us all look out here by the main road if you didn't lose it out here?" one man asked.

"My house only provides light from a single window. Out here I get full light from the sun. It is much easier to see. When I'm inside my house, I cannot see because it is clouded with shadows."

"You make no sense, Malariba. We cannot find something on this road if you have not lost it on this road. It is simply not here," a kind lady villager spoke. She didn't want to be harsh with Malariba, who was a respected elder.

Malariba broke out into a hearty laugh. It was so loud that it echoed over the neighbouring lands and far into the distance.

"You all believe you are so smart don't you? But you have much to learn. When are you going to use your common sense for the things that really matter in your lives?"

All Eyes stayed focused on the old wise woman. The villagers were confused and tried to figure out this situation. Malariba raised her hand and slowly made eye contact with everybody around her. Malariba had very compelling eyes that drew people in.

"Every one of you must stop focusing on getting more of everything. Toys, money and shiny stones do not provide happiness. Yet, all you seem to be concerned about are material objects and proving yourself better than your fellow man. Still, you cannot understand why you are unhappy. Nobody can be happy when they are focused on fighting, bickering and complaining. It is not in our spirit to be that way." Malariba explained.

Some villagers began to understand and looked down to the ground, feeling very ashamed. While others looked scornfully at the old woman because they refuse to believe her words.

Malariba continued to speak, "You have been focusing on getting everything you do not need and everything that you do need has left your hearts. You trade competitiveness for happiness. You want to be a lone winner more than a member of this village. Don't you realise that until your happiness and fulfilment comes from the inside you will never be content? True happiness is not won in a competition; it can only develop when you begin appreciating what is around you and what provides your heart true joy and serenity."

The villagers sullenly looked at each other like children who had just been scorned for causing trouble. They knew the wise old woman spoke the truth for they could feel it in their hearts. They also knew not to engage in arguments with the elders so they kept silent.

"Why do you all search for your own precious gems outside? They are not there. They are to be there. found within you. You are the gem that should be protected by you. These competitive ways will destroy your precious spirit and inner shine. Just remember, you need to find a way to be content from within to live a truly fulfilling life."

"Help us, Malariba," the villagers cried. "We did not realize."

"Well then, stop all this nonsense. If your inner self is a dark and unknown place, make it your job to get to know it and brighten it up." Malariba turned to her hut and continued her hearty laugh.

At that very moment, the stars in the sky shone brightly. Night had already fallen. Under those stars the villagers all agreed that they would stop their foolish competing and bickering ways. They had learned that what was truly important did not come from the outside, nor did it come in shiny, glittering packages. It came from deep within.

After that evening, wonderful things began to happen once again in the village. It became one of the happiest places in the entire Kingdom and its joy rang across the plains.

THE END

OR MAYBE NOT JUST YET…

SEE NEXT PAGES

Check if any more Books in The Legends of Altai series is available

www.legendsofaltai.com

STUDENT, READER WORKBOOK

STORY: 1
The King and the Miraculous Healing

What have you learned?
Write a few sentences about what this story teaches you.

_____
_____
_____
_____
_____
_____
_____
_____
_____
_____

My New Words

Write the definition for all of the words listed. Once this task is completed, write a phrase that contains the word.

Deformed

_____
_____
_____

Humble

_____
_____
_____

Unfavourable

_____
_____
_____

Physician

_____
_____
_____

Heir

_____
_____
_____

Intent

_____
_____
_____

Contemplation.

_____
_____
_____

ACTIVITIES – MY EXPEREINCE

Setting Goals Exercise

Did you set goals for yourself? What are they? My Goals are:

_____
_____
_____

_____
_____
_____
_____

What was easy about it and what was hard?
_____
_____
_____
_____
_____
_____

Dreaming the Dream Exercise

What are your dreams? Were you surprised?
_____
_____
_____
_____
_____
_____

The Miracle Exercise

Do you think your miracle can come true? Why or why not?

Outside Visit

Write a few sentences about who you met and what you learnt.

_____
_____
_____
_____
_____
_____
_____
_____
_____
_____
_____
_____
_____
_____
_____

Story Board

Is there anyone in your life that is going through something similar to what is happening in the story?

_____
_____
_____
_____

A Few Questions
How does this story make you feel? Why?

_____
_____
_____
_____

What is the part you like most? Why?

_____
_____
_____
_____

What is the part that you like the least? Why?

_____
_____
_____
_____

How could the lesson learned in this Story affect and benefit your life?

_____
_____
_____
_____

What is a simple action, behaviour that you could implement straight away in your life?

_____
_____
_____
_____

Describe how this lesson could be used to benefit your relationships with others and study:

_____
_____
_____
_____

Describe how this lesson could be used to benefit your future:

_____
_____
_____
_____

Is there anyone in your life that is going through something similar to what is happening in the story?

_____
_____
_____
_____

STORY: 2
The King and the Beggar

Write a few sentences about what this story teaches you.

My New Words

Write the definition for all of the words listed. Once this task is completed, write a phrase that contains the word.

Productive

_____
_____
_____

Gracious

_____
_____
_____

Pouring

_____
_____
_____

Wondered

_____

_____
_____

Contentment
_____
_____
_____

Existence
_____
_____
_____

Contribution
_____
_____
_____

Activities - My Experience

Art Work
Draw the illustration with the King and Maya in front of the Beggar.

_____
_____
_____
_____
_____
_____

Role Play
One person Plays the King the other the Beggar

_____
_____
_____
_____
_____
_____
_____
_____

A Few Questions

How does this story make you feel? Why?

_____
_____
_____
_____

What is the part you like most? Why?

_____
_____
_____
_____

What is the part that you like the least? Why?

_____
_____
_____
_____
_____
_____

How could the lesson learned in this Story affect and benefit your life?

_____
_____
_____

What is a simple action, behaviour that you could implement straight away in your life?

_____
_____
_____

Describe how this lesson could be used to benefit your relationships with others and study:

_____
_____
_____

Describe how this lesson could be used to benefit your future:

_____
_____
_____

Is there anyone in your life that is going through something similar to what is happening in the story?

_____
_____
_____
_____
_____
_____
_____

STORY: 3
King Ultan and his 3 Sons

Write a few sentences about what this story teaches you.

My New Words

Write the definition for all of the words listed. Once this task is completed, write a phrase that contains the word.

Justice

_____
_____
_____

Leadership

_____
_____
_____

Secured

_____
_____
_____

Comprised

_____
_____
_____

Intended

_____
_____
_____
_____

Ornamental

_____
_____
_____
_____

Other Word #1:

_____
_____
_____
_____

Other Word #2:

_____
_____
_____
_____

ACTIVITIES

Art Work

Create a colour drawing of your favourite scene in this story.

_____
_____
_____
_____

Practical Task/Project

How many species did you identify?

_____
_____
_____
_____
_____
_____
_____
_____

Writing Activity

Did you agree with King Ultan's choice? Why or why not? ?

_____
_____
_____
_____
_____
_____
_____
_____
_____
_____
_____
_____
_____
_____
_____

A Few Questions

How does this story make you feel? Why?
_____
_____

What is the part you like most? Why?
_____
_____
_____

What is the part that you like the least? Why?
_____
_____
_____

How could the lesson learned in this Story affect and benefit your life?
_____
_____
_____

_____
_____
_____
_____

What is a simple action, behaviour that you could implement straight away in your life?

_____
_____
_____

Describe how this lesson could be used to benefit your relationships with others and study:

_____
_____
_____

Describe how this lesson could be used to benefit your future:

Is there anyone in your life that is going through something similar to what is happening in the story?

STORY: 4
Looking Inside

Write a few sentences about what this story teaches you.

My New Words

Write the definition for all of the words listed. Once this task is completed, write a phrase that contains the word.

To count on

_____
_____
_____
_____

Hostility

_____
_____
_____
_____

Competitive

_____
_____
_____
_____

Compelling
_____
_____
_____

Savannah
_____
_____
_____

Respected
_____
_____
_____

Extra Word:
_____
_____
_____

Activities

Inner Resources Exercise
What inner resources did you did discover?

_____
_____
_____
_____
_____
_____
_____
_____
_____
_____
_____
_____

Art Work

What did you draw and/or paint?

_____
_____
_____

Writing Activity

Who did you invite and why?

_____
_____
_____
_____
_____
_____
_____
_____

How could the lesson learned in this Story affect and benefit your life?

_____
_____
_____
_____
_____
_____
_____
_____

A Few Questions

How does this story make you feel? Why?

_____
_____
_____
_____

What is the part you like most? Why?

_____
_____
_____

What is the part that you like the least? Why?

_____
_____
_____

How could the lesson learned in this Story affect and benefit your life?

_____
_____
_____

What is a simple action, behaviour that you could implement straight away in your life?

_____
_____
_____

Describe how this lesson could be used to benefit your relationships with others and study:

_____
_____
_____

Describe how this lesson could be used to benefit your future:

_____
_____
_____

Is there anyone in your life that is going through something similar to what is happening in the story?

_____
_____
_____

COLOURING BOOK

King Argoz   Xavier the Wise

TEACHERS AND PARENTS WORK BOOK

Introduction

This handbook is a guide to the first book in the Legends of Altai book series.

As a teacher, you have the opportunity of being able to encourage a young mind to develop value and respect for all life. These stories have been written to showcase life values and the greatness of life potential to children.

It is hoped that this book will help you as a teacher to open the eyes of your students to the wonders of nature – the majesty of the seas, the puzzles of the heavens, the complexities of human emotions – in all their myriad forms. In fact, feelings and empathetic re-creation of feelings form the basis of most of the exercises in this handbook.

If you are a using this book as a parent, then it's worth remembering that none of us was given a manual at the start of our parenthood, and so most of us struggle along trying to survive as best we can. Some of the exercises are not applicable to very small groups, but those that most suitable are marked with this symbol . Another very powerful way to use the guide is to prompt discussions between yourself and your child or children.

If you are using this book in a classroom setting, you may wish to incorporate the exercises into your own lesson plan. Ideas for lesson plans are given with each tale, along with a summary of the main point/wisdom lesson. Some of the exercises may be carried out of the school into the broader society. This is because one of the great messages of the stories is that we live in an interconnected world, and that what happens to one part of the world happens to all of it.

The most important thing, wither in the classroom or at home, is to create an atmosphere of trust and acceptance. Plan the time carefully but allow for spontaneity as well.

Perhaps the greatest gift we can give children is to empower their imagination. We are born with a rich inner world which in the past has often been crushed by overly rigid systems of tuition and discipline. But the inner life is a great resource which, if properly encouraged and trained, will feed a person's spirit for a whole lifetime.

The stories have a personal slant in that I believe that divine presence is in all beings. However, we live a diverse society with a great range of religions and so references to God have been made more neutral – as The Great One. The aim is always to teach without preaching, and to show without prescribing.

Although the Workbook is aimed at children, it is relevant to us all.

You might want to Award the Diploma (Template in Appendix) to each child as a final touch to round off the experience of reading the book.

Please enjoy the Tales and any feedback is welcomed.

How to Use this Book

For Teachers

How you use this guide and the stories depends on your understanding of your students. Another important factor is the age of the students themselves and also their grasp of the English language.

If the students do not speak English as their first language, or if you are using the stories in an ESL context, then you may wish to use some of the vocabulary, language activities first before moving onto the life lessons/wisdom aspects of each story. There is a useful list of questions which you can use to initiate discussions or set essay topics in Appendix 1.

Suggestions are given for activities which will focus the student's enjoyment of the story, leading to an understanding and internalisation of the life lessons and wisdom contained each one of them. You may wish to adapt the activities according the age and abilities of the class.

For Parents

How you use this guide will depend on the age of your child/children. You may want to re-enforce new vocabulary and spelling as a lead-in to the story, or you may want to just read the story to them and ask them what they have understood by listening to it. There is a useful list of questions which you can use to initiate discussions in Appendix 1

One way to integrate the life lesson/wisdom is to relate it to everyday experience. For example, if someone has judged another person recently and not shown compassion, you could ask your child how things could be different if peoples' attitudes changed.

The important thing to remember is that you can't get it wrong as long as you keep an open channel of dialogue between yourself and your child. Reflect on the lessons for yourself and be prepared to change your own mind!

STORY 1

The King and the Miraculous Healing

Summary of the Life lesson/Wisdom

If you ask you'll be given. However you have to ask sincerely and humbly. If you truly believe in miracles, there is nothing stopping you. Your mind and your imagination is the greatest tool you have at your disposal to enhance your life. If you believe you can't you will not do it, if you believe you can, you can!

Lesson Plan

Lead in by asking the children what they would change about themselves.

Pre-teach vocabulary and ask students to note it in their books.

Tell the children the title of the story and ask them to predict what the life lesson will be. Ask them if they know the word miracle and whether they believe in them.

Read the story – or ask the class to read paragraphs of it in turn.

Ask the students to do some of the activities.

Finish by asking the children if they know of any miracles. Explain that many miracles start small, or unnoticed and that it may take time to manifest. You might like to close out the lesson with The *Miracle Exercise* to round the lesson off.

Ask the students what they think it means and guide them towards the summary of the life lesson – and maybe other points they will see in the story.

Ask the students to do some of the activities.

Ask the students to reflect on people they dislike. It is quite challenging for students to come out with people they dislike that are actually present, so it might be an idea for them to describe other people. You could set the scene by talking about a person you didn't like but came to understand better by understanding their circumstances.

Pre-teach Vocabulary

Deformed, humble, unfavourable, physician, heir, intent, contemplation.

Activities

Setting Goals Exercise

It's never too early to encourage people to set goals. Ask the children to write down what they would like to achieve by the end of the term. It's a good idea to share some of your previous goals with them, and maybe a little bit about how you achieved them.

Remind them that goals must be measurable to be effective. So 'my goal is arithmetic to improve' would not be measurable. But 'my goal is to always get 70% or more for in arithmetic tests' would be.

Remember to get the children to re-visit the goals at the end of term and see how much progress has been made. A nice way to do this is to have each child write their goal on a slip of paper and put in an envelop. Post the envelopes on a class board with the heading 'Our Goals'. On the last day of term, get the children to open their own envelope and see how much progress they have made.

Dreaming the Dream Exercise

Move the discussion away from physical characteristics and outward things like houses, cars etc and ask the children what dreams they would like to come true. Ask them to write them down. Explain that you have to hold steadfast to your dream for a period of time, that change isn't always instant. Focus on small but measurable changes eg improving my spelling, reading more fluently.

Explain that whatever you focus on in your life tends to become more dominant. So if you say to yourself 'I'll never be able to spell well', that tends to be your experience. Show them the positive way 'My spelling's getting better and better each day.'

The Miracle Exercise

Ask the children what who represent a miracle in their lives. Answers will be very varied. Try to steer the conversation away from material goods, and more towards personal goals. Then ask them to imagine that the miracle has already happened and the change has taken place when they were asleep.

Ask the miracle question – how do you know the miracle has taken place? Answers will usually be able feeling things are different. Ask the children to take that feeling and try to already feel it. Feeling the feelings really helps to create the miracle! (Adapted from Solution-Focused Counselling)

Outside Visit

Although this story is about physical deformity being corrected it is really about so much more. Sometimes the most healed and healing spirits live in bodies that seem less than perfect.

If this possible, arrange a visit to a home for physically disabled people. It can be quite remarkable how uplifting this can be in the right circumstances though it will probably require research and exploration to find the right place and right people.

Story Board

Divide the children into groups of three or four. Give each group a story board (a template for this is included in the appendix) and ask them to tell the story in words and pictures.

It's a good idea to blow the story board up to A3 size so the children have plenty of room. It's also an idea to cut out some of the drawing rectangles so that some children can be working on the drawings while others in the group are preparing the written work.

STORY 2

The King and the Beggar

Summary of the Life lesson/Wisdom

Life is a reflection of your inner Mind Set. The Mind cannot be satisfied, look deeper to find lasting peace, beyond the peak and valleys of the ego.

Lesson Plan

Start by drawing a glass on the whiteboard half full of water. Ask the class whether it is half full or half empty. Ask the class whether those things mean the same thing.

Write the following on the board *Kng rgz nd th wsdm f th bl vlt*. Be prepared to explain that the vowels are missing – can the children guess them. This little exercise stretches the mind and encourages people to think beyond the limitations of a situation.

Pre-teach vocabulary and ask students to note it in their books.

Read out the title of the story and ask the students to guess what the story is about. What is a blue violet? Can it exist? Stretch their minds.

Read the story – or ask the class to read paragraphs of it in turn.

Ask the students to do some of the activities.

Ask the students to reflect on what limits people. You might want to open up the subject of differently abled people here, or just different gifts around the class. You could round off the lesson by doing a mingle exercise in which students go around the room telling other students what their gift is.

Pre-teach Vocabulary

Productive, Gracious, Pouring, Wondered, Contentment, Existence, Contribution, Recognition

Activities

Word Search

Use the wordsearch below or use a Word Search program (easily available on the internet, try http://puzzlemaker.discoveryeducation.com/) to generate new words or words that children have difficulty spelling. They then have to find the letters in a jumble and this helps their minds focus on the actual letters.

STORY 3

The King Argoz and his 3 Sons

Summary of the Life lesson/Wisdom

You can unlock the gift of life. Everyone has special Gifts, Talents and something worth sharing. Everyone has a special place in this life. The best way to deal with love or life is to share it. Individuals will deal with life differently.

The more we think outside the box and find solutions that do not only benefit us but everyone, the more we will be able to support life, others and ourselves. Try to find a win/win situation when you are faced with choices. It does not matter if the recipient recognizes your effort. It's about you knowing that your choices can make a difference.

Lesson Plan

Lead in to the lesson by talking about the power of choice. Give an example from your own life where you have had to make a choice. Ask when you make a choice is it important to consider the impact on other people or not?

Pre-teach vocabulary and ask students to note it in their books.

Tell the children the title of the story and ask them to predict what the life lesson will be.

Read the story – or ask the class to read paragraphs of it in turn.

Ask the students to do some of the activities.

Round off the lesson by asking the children if they would have chosen Ryan over Aaron or Niall. Why?

Pre-teach Vocabulary

Justice, leadership, secured, comprised, intended, ornamental, generated

Activities

Art Work

Ask the children to make a plan or a drawing of Prince Ryan's garden. Tell them to include as many species as they can.

Practical Task/Project

Tell the children to collect as many seeds as they can. Then using reference books or the Internet, to identify what the seeds will grow into. Make a display in the class of the seed and the fully grown plant. This exercise is a reflection on the power of nature to create abundant life from a tiny beginning.

Writing Activity

Write a report on what each of the three princes did with his portion of the seeds. What are the positive and negative aspects of each choice? You might want to go through the basics of report writing – balance and fairness and an overall, reasoned conclusion. Ask the children whether or not they agree with King Ultan's choice. Why/Why not?

Writing/Drawing Project

Create a class newspaper. One way of doing this is to divide the task up so that everybody has something to do. Take a huge sheet of paper and cut up lots of smaller pieces of paper for headlines, articles and pictures. Bring some examples of an actual newspaper into the class. Dramatise the event of the King returning to the Kingdom. There could be a story about what he did when he was away, news about each of the three sons initiatives, obituaries, other news items, weather etc.

STORY 4

Looking Inside

Summary of the Life lesson/Wisdom

True happiness resides within. We can buy as many new toys as we desire. But these will not give us long lasting happiness and fulfilment. Life is not about 'keeping up with the Jones' is about being truly fulfilled and happy within, than no matter what happens in the outside we will be stable, balanced and fulfilled.

Lesson Plan

Lead in by asking the class where happiness comes from – inside or outside? What creates inner happiness? Introduce the topic of personal assets/resources eg courage, intelligence, kindness etc.

Pre-teach vocabulary and ask students to note it in their books.

Tell the children the title of the story and ask them to predict what the life lesson will be.

Read the story – or ask the class to read paragraphs of it in turn.

Ask the students to do some of the activities.

Round off the class by asking the children what they have learnt by reading all the stories in the book. You might like to award them the Diploma, see resource in Appendix area.

Pre-teach Vocabulary

To count on, hostility, competitive, compelling, savannah, respected

Activities

Inner Resource Exercise

Start by talking about the difference between inner and outer resources. For this activity focus on inner personal resources or assets eg kindness, courage, intelligence, creativity etc.

Then using the template Gallery of My Assets, ask each child to fill it in for themselves. They could write the asset or draw a picture of it. You could broaden this out to include family/friends as assets.

Art Work

What did Malariba see when she looked out of her window?

Writing Activity #1

Write a letter from one of the villagers about Malariba coming to live in the village. It could include any details about Malariba that have been introduced in earlier stories and other examples of the things she has done to help the villagers.

You might want to give them a template for this or some examples to work from. The Certificate should include the qualities that are most noteworthy in the child's eyes, so you may want to brainstorm a list of possibilities on the board eg kind, gentle, good cook, encouraging etc

Writing Activity #2

Maya had an interesting life – write her biography. Divide the task up into groups – one write about her early life, one about her life on the streets, one about meeting the king and being adopted into the royal family etc. Maybe there are other episodes that are not covered which the class could create?

Writing/Drawing Project

Write a fan book (template provided in Appendix) or else find a template for a mini book on the Internet. Include as much of the story as the children can remember – and encourage illustrations.

Appendix 1:

Questions to ask about each story

How does this story make you feel? Why?

What is the part you like most? Why?

What is the part that you like the least? Why?

How could the lesson learned in this Story affect and benefit your life?

What is a simple action, behaviour that you could implement straight away in your life?

Describe how this lesson could be used to benefit your relationships:

Describe how this lesson could be used to benefit your study/work:

Describe how this lesson could be used to benefit your future:

Is there anyone in your life that is going through something similar to what is happening in the story?

Appendix 2:

GALLERY OF ASSETS

Appendix 3: Princess Maya's Window

Appendix 4: Certificate of Achievement

SHARE THE MESSAGE

These stories changed my life as a child and continue to do so every day. Every time I read or reflect upon them, I find a new message or a layer of meaning. I would love to hear about the impact these tales have had in your lives. Have they changed a hard situation? Did they inspire you to make a stand? Perhaps, they have simply touched you and reminded you of the important things in life.

I welcome you to share your testimonials with me and would be honoured to hear what you have to say. If you have a personal story you believe could fit in the series, please let me know. I always welcome the gift of wisdom and any opportunity to share it. You may contact me at:

www.legendsofaltai.com/pages/share.php

KEEPING IN TOUCH

- If you are interested in future books, please join our **mailing list** by visiting: www.legendsofaltai.com/pages/keep-in-touch.php

- Visit the official *Legends of Altai* **website** : www.legendsofaltai.com and bookmark it for future reference.

YOU CAN MAKE A DIFFERENCE!

You can play an important role in fanning the winds of change around the globe. You have the power to start this change within your own family, neighbourhood, city, state, country and the world. It all starts with you. It continues by letting others know what you've discovered. Let's start a revolution of self-discovery!

I truly hope to create a lasting ritual of bedtime stories that contain wisdom and inspiration. If we give just a little more, our world will see many amazing moments from simple small gestures.

It can start with you...

Spreading the word is easy and free. It can be an incredible rewarding experience.

Below are some of the few things you could do to truly make a difference in someone life, school, community and state.

- Share a **free chapter** with your friends: Chapter 7: "King Ultan and his 3 Sons" can be downloaded to share: www.legendsofaltai.com/pages/free-gifts.php

- A good way to spread this message is to ask your **local school & library** to obtain this book and/or the rest of the series.

- Couldn't find a copy of this book at your **local book-store**? Then ask about it! Most book-stores will order copies if requested.

- If you are part of a **book club**, please mention how this book has inspired you.

- Give the book as a Birthday or Christmas present.

- Speak with your school Principal or teachers in regards to making this book part of the **curriculum or school library**.

- Use the book bulk discount (on the site) and offer the book as a **Fund-Raising** product. (Under the Bookstores, Schools & Libraries link on the site)

- Write a **blog, articles** about your experience with the Legends of Altai and submit it to your web site or local newspaper.

- Let your friends and family know about the Lewgends of Altai through your **Facebook**

- Let your friends and family know about the Lewgends of Altai through your **Twitter**

ANY HELP IN SPREADING THE WORD ABOUT THIS BOOK IS APPRECIATED!

I wish you all the very best your mind and heart can conceive.
Paolo F. Tiberi

WHOLESALE & PRIVATE LABEL EDITIONS

Buy in bulk/wholesale for your
fund-raiser, institution, school
(Workbook for Students and Teacher
Reference Book also Available)

For more information visit:
www.legendsofaltai.com/pages/bookstores_libraries.php

Arrange a "Special Edition – Private Label" of
this book for your company, organisation,
or association with your own
personalised message.
(Minimum orders apply.)
www.legendsofaltai.com/pages/contact.php

Book the Author for an Event

Paolo F. Tiberi is a successful entrepreneur, published author, public speaker, educator and motivator. He was invited to speak at several television shows in Italy and had his own program in a small regional television channel in Rome before deciding to move to Australia.

There, he was invited to speak and inspire the unemployed people at the Salvation Army Employment Plus and had a 30-minute segment on Radio Italia, an Italian radio station broadcasting to 250,000 Australia wide.

To read the inspirational full life story of Paolo visit:
http://www.paolotiberi.com/pages/paolo_tiberi.html

Special Thanks

The best creative processes use great minds to make a work not only stand out, but stand apart. This book, with its precious stories, has been developed by ancient parables. Many of these stories are hundreds, even thousands, of years old. English is not my mother tongue, so my beautiful wife, Abigail Tiberi, has been so gracious to help make the stories more interesting and rich, using much of her free time to support this project. She also assisted in modifying my English whenever necessary.

A very special thanks also goes to all the devoted individuals who have helped editing and proof reading the stories in this book. These individuals are Ramona Resurreccion, Margaret Preller Osako, Megan Peterson Morrow and Jillian McKellan, they have been of great assistance in regards to the readability of what you hold in your hands today.

The front cover mountain ranges has been modified from a picture taken by Ondrej Žvácek. The castle in the distance is a modified version of Kishi Church taken by Matthias Kabel. I thank all of them for taking those pictures.

I offer my fondest thanks to all the teachers, people, places and events that have made me the person I am today. They have all given me a little more wisdom than I would have otherwise not have experienced. Each day I discover more, I learn more and realize that I still have much more to learn. Knowledge is a lifetime quest that I embrace with a passion.

And a final and most appreciative thank you goes to <u>YOU the reader</u>, for having invested in this book. I am thankful that you are taking the time to enjoy the stories and the knowledge and wisdom they contain.

NOTES

NOTES

NOTES

NOTES

NOTES

www.ingramcontent.com/pod-product-compliance
Lightning Source LLC
LaVergne TN
LVHW051840080426
835512LV00018B/2991